Did You

CORNWALL

A MISCELLANY

Compiled by Julia Skinner

With particular reference to the work of Martin Dunning,
Des Hannigan, Bob Richards, Terence Sackett and Peter Stanier

THE FRANCIS FRITH COLLECTION

www.francisfrith.com

First published in the United Kingdom in 2010 by The Francis Frith Collection®

This edition published exclusively for Bradwell Books in 2012
For trade enquiries see: www.bradwellbooks.com or tel: 0800 834 920
ISBN 978-1-84589-542-6

Text and Design copyright The Francis Frith Collection®
Photographs copyright The Francis Frith Collection® except where indicated.

The Frith® photographs and the Frith® logo are reproduced under licence from
Heritage Photographic Resources Ltd, the owners of the Frith® archive and trademarks.
'The Francis Frith Collection', 'Francis Frith' and 'Frith' are registered trademarks of
Heritage Photographic Resources Ltd.

British Library Cataloguing in Publication Data

Did You Know? Cornwall - A Miscellany
Compiled by Julia Skinner
With particular reference to the work of Martin Dunning, Des Hannigan, Bob Richards,
Terence Sackett and Peter Stanier

The Francis Frith Collection
Oakley Business Park,
Wylye Road, Dinton,
Wiltshire SP3 5EU
Tel: +44 (0) 1722 716 376
Email: info@francisfrith.co.uk
www.francisfrith.com

Printed and bound in Malaysia
Contains material sourced from responsibly managed forests

Front Cover: **POLPERRO, THE HARBOUR 1924** 7633lp
Frontispiece: **TRURO, CALENICK VILLAGE 1912** 64745

The colour-tinting is for illustrative purposes only, and is not intended to be historically accurate

CONTENTS

INTRODUCTION

Crossing the River Tamar into Cornwall brings travellers the impression that they are entering a foreign land. Cornwall, England's most westerly county, is a unique treasure house of Celtic language, myth and legend, a heritage proudly maintained by Cornish people. Cornwall's perceived 'difference' from the rest of England can be ascribed to several factors: its geographical isolation, its hard granite backbone and its ancient mineral wealth. Of even greater significance is the fact that Cornwall is surrounded by sea on three sides and nowhere in the county is more than twenty miles from the coast. In this beautiful but harsh landscape Cornish people made their living in perilous ways in the past: from the sea as fishermen, sailors and smugglers, and from the land in farming and the mineral and china clay industries. Both trades encouraged a toughness of spirit and strong local and regional pride.

The estuaries of the Tamar, Fowey, Fal, Helston and Camel rivers bite far inland, and provided valuable water highways in the past. Along the county's long coastline, the many inlets and coves formed small harbours and ports and were a lifeline for trade and Cornwall's once-great fishing industry. Inland, the hard granite rocks of Cornwall have yielded an unsurpassed mineral wealth over the centuries – tin, copper, lead, zinc and other metals, hewn from deep mines. Towns such as Redruth and Camborne grew up around the mining industry, and powerful mine-owners such as Joseph Thomas Treffry bought and developed whole harbours in order to ship copper ores to the smelters of South Wales. Granite and slate were also quarried and exported from small harbours along the coast, at places such as Tintagel, Port Gaverne and Port Isaac, and china clay from the St Austell area. Dairying and stock grazing on Cornish farms have always been important, and the mild climate, influenced by the surrounding sea, has allowed for crops of early potatoes and other vegetables such as broccoli, and also for flowers, especially daffodils.

Cornwall's great industrial glories, however, now seem all in the past. By the late 1800s its massive fishing industry was already in decline, and today Cornwall's harbours are almost empty of working ships. Its mines are disused and only the quarrying of china clay has continued to expand since its origins in the late 1700s. Throughout the county there is evidence of lost prosperity and fallen industrial might: the remains of mine shafts, quarry workings and tramways can be found in many places, and the gaunt ruins of disused engine houses stand watch over lonely cliff tops and moorland. Cornwall is perhaps now better known for its industrial archaeology than its living industry.

Cornwall now relies on tourism for much of its economic well-being, but although it is constantly under siege each summer from thousands of visitors who invade its roads, towns and villages, it is still possible to trace Cornwall's unique essence around its quiet backwaters and many wide river estuaries, its lonely moors and along its dramatic coast. It is a county dearly loved by inhabitants and visitors alike.

POLPERRO, THE HARBOUR 1888 21270

CORNISH DIALECT WORDS

'Aglets' – Hawthorn berries.

'Bulhorns' – snails.

'Emmets' or **'murrians'** – ants. Nowadays both words are also used for tourists.

'Flam-new' – brand new.

'Grammersow' – a woodlouse.

'Steeved' – very cold, frozen through.

'Ploffy' – plump.

'Teasy' – bad-tempered.

'Urts' – whortleberries, or bilberries.

'Kernow' – the name for Cornwall in 'Kernewek', the old Celtic Cornish language which is closely related to both Breton and Welsh. It died out as a mother tongue in the 1770s, but still lives on in thousands of place-names. An old rhyme says 'By Tre, Pol and Pen, Ye shall know Cornishmen', and these are the most common prefixes in Cornish place-names: 'Tre' means homestead or town, 'Pol' means pool, and 'Pen' means headland or hill. Other common prefixes in Cornish place-names are 'Porth' (meaning bay), 'Lan' (denoting an early religious enclosure, later the site of a church) and 'Ros' (meaning heath).

MENHENIOT, MEN 1912 64607x

HAUNTED CORNWALL

One of Cornwall's most famous ghosts is that of Jan Tregeagle. In his earthly life in the 17th century he was a stern and unpopular local magistrate, notorious for his corrupt ways. Many crimes, including murdering his wife and children, have been ascribed to him in folklore and it is not known for sure whether they are all true, but his reputation was so black that it was widely believed that he had sold his soul to the Devil. Ghost tales and legends featuring Jan Tregeagle are found all over Cornwall, but his phantom is particularly linked with Bodmin Moor, where his despairing cries can be heard on the wind as the Devil relentlessly pursues him over the moor with a pack of headless hounds, trying to catch Tregeagle and claim his soul.

Cornish miners were very superstitious, and were always careful not to offend the underground spirits they called 'knockers' which they believed haunted the galleries of the mines. The knockers were usually helpful and would make tapping, or knocking, noises in the mines to guide the miners to rich seams of ore, but if the spirits heard anyone whistling, or if the miners refused to appease them with offerings of food or wax from their lanterns, they would cause rock falls and other accidents.

Another of Cornwall's famous ghosts is the shade of Charlotte Dymond, who was found murdered on the slopes of Rough Tor, near Camelford, on 14th April 1844. Her lover was tried for her murder and hanged at Bodmin Jail, but there is some doubt that he was guilty. Charlotte's ghost is said to roam around the area where she was killed, dressed in a long gown, a red shawl and an old-fashioned bonnet; her presence is particularly active around the anniversary of her death. The site of her murder is marked with a memorial stone, and her story inspired 'The Ballad of Charlotte Dymond' by the Cornish poet Charles Causley.

STRATTON, SANCTUARY 1906 56089

CORNWALL MISCELLANY

Beneath the granite tor of weathered overhanging slabs on Bodmin Moor known as the Cheesewring is a small cave-house that was once the home of a local stonecutter, Daniel Gumb, in which he brought up at least 9 children. On a stone beside the house is carved 'D GUMB 1735', believed to be the date of Daniel's third marriage – potential wives were obviously not put off by the unusual living arrangements!

LISKEARD, THE CHEESEWRING 1890 24476

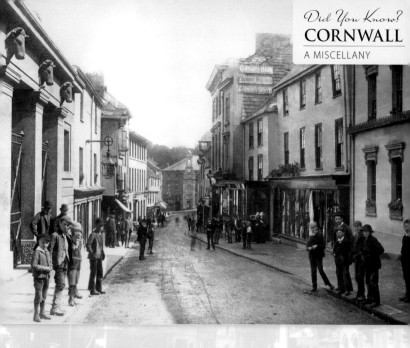

BODMIN, FORE STREET 1890 24482

The Market House in Bodmin's Fore Street was built in 1839-40 for the sale of meat, poultry and butter, and the four carved ox heads above the pillars are a notable feature of the street's frontage (see photograph 24482, above).

The forbidding buildings of the former County Jail stand on the northern edge of the town of Bodmin, now a visitor attraction. During the First World War, the Crown Jewels and the Domesday Book were sent there for safekeeping.

One of Cornwall's famous holy wells is St Keyne's Well in the East Looe valley. St Keyne is said to have bestowed a special power on this well, that whichever one of a newly-married couple drank its water before the other would be the master of the marriage.

Cornwall's tin and copper deposits have been exploited since ancient times, and there is evidence that the Phoenicians were making the long sea journey to Cornwall to trade for tin as early as 500BC. The county's mineral wealth was important in the development of many of its towns – Liskeard's prosperity, for instance, was originally due to the copper mines at Caradon Hill.

During the Civil War most of Cornwall was fiercely Royalist. St Neot still has a tradition of showing its loyalty to the Royalist cause by keeping an oak branch on the top of the tower of its parish church; a new branch is placed there each year on Oak Apple Day, (29th May), a former public holiday that celebrated Charles II's restoration to the throne in 1660.

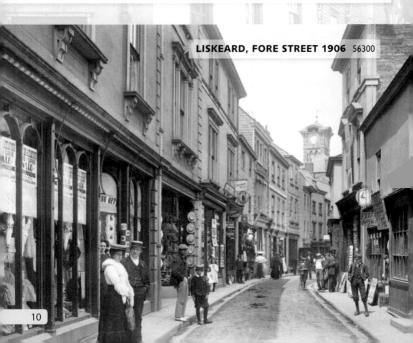

LISKEARD, FORE STREET 1906 56300

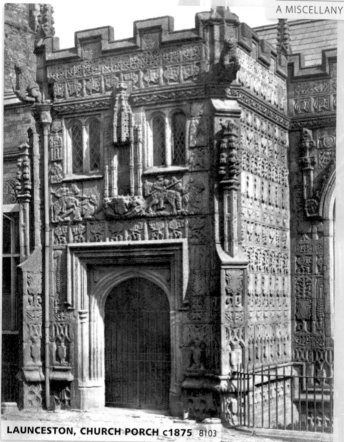

LAUNCESTON, CHURCH PORCH c1875 8103

The exterior of St Mary's Church in Launceston is covered with beautifully carved designs, figures and foliage, including a depiction of St George and the dragon on the south porch. Below the chancel window on the north side of the church is a figure of St Mary Magdalene to whom the church is dedicated – a pebble thrown onto her back is said to bring good luck.

LOSTWITHIEL, ON THE ROAD TO RESTORMEL HOUSE 1906 56431

The Fowey River winds down to the sea from Lostwithiel to Fowey. Lostwithiel was once a major port, but silting of the river brought this to an end. On a slope above Lostwithiel are the ruins of Restormel Castle, and there is much of interest to see in the town, including the old Duchy Palace, the remains of the quays, and the octagonal spire of the 14th-century church of St Bartholomew.

An ancient route crossing Cornwall from north to south is known today as the Saints' Way, and used as a long-distance walking trail. In the past it was a route followed by pilgrims from Ireland and Wales who crossed the Bristol Channel to land at Padstow, and then walked across Cornwall to Fowey to take ship for Europe, thus avoiding the dangerous sea voyage around Land's End.

The King of Prussia pub on Town Quay in Fowey is named after an 18th-century smuggler, John Carter. West of Praa Sands, between Helston and Penzance, is Prussia Cove, a narrow inlet which John Carter ran as his own fiefdom – he even mounted a battery of guns on the cliff. This gave him the nickname of 'The King of Prussia'.

Daphne du Maurier's novel 'Rebecca' famously begins 'Last night I dreamt I went to Manderley again'. The author lived at the great house of Menabilly near Fowey from 1943-1967, and the house was the inspiration for 'Manderley' in her book.

The quirky name of Readymoney Cove near Fowey conjures up images of smugglers, but it probably derives from an earlier name of 'Redemen', meaning a pebble ford.

FOWEY, FROM HALL WALK 1901 47696

MEVAGISSEY, THE HARBOUR
A FISHING BOAT 1898 41398A

The pilchard catch was the most important to Cornish fishermen in the past. Pilchards are full-grown specimens of sardines, and huge shoals of these fish used to swarm around the coast. They would be fished by up to fifty boats operating in unison to ring the shoal with their seine nets. Vast quantities of pilchards used to be salted for export and to feed the Royal Navy, which considered the pilchard fishery so important that in the 18th century the Admiralty released an edict that no pilchard men were to be taken by the press gangs for naval service. Pilchards caught by Mevagissey's huge fishing fleet were supplied dried to the Royal Navy and were known as 'Mevagissey Ducks.'

Among the monuments in St Nonna's Church in Pelynt is one to the local man Sir Jonathan Trelawny, Bishop of Bristol, who was sent to the Tower of London by James II for petitioning against the Declaration of Indulgence in 1687. His arrest is the subject of the Cornish folksong with the refrain: 'And shall Trelawney die? Here's 20,000 Cornishmen shall know the reason why.' Trelawny was held for three weeks before being released, an event celebrated with church bells being rung in Pelynt.

In the 1740s the properties of Cornwall's china clay and china stone for porcelain manufacturing were discovered, and from the 1770s the Staffordshire Potteries took an interest in the St Austell area. The china clay industry dates from that time, and over the years the whole landscape of the region has been remodelled by Cornwall's major extractive industry. Quarrying the china clay has created a strange lunar landscape of huge waste tips of sand, gravel and rock around St Austell, which has given the area the name of the 'Cornish Alps'.

ST AUSTELL, FORE STREET 1912 64750

The tower of St Austell's 15th-century parish church of Holy Trinity is one of the finest in Cornwall, and its west side is notable for a series of carved figures depicting the Trinity, the Annunciation and the Resurrection.

A feature of the Luxulyan valley near St Blazey is the magnificent 1839 Treffry viaduct and aqueduct, carrying both a tramway and a water course, which linked the mining and china clay industries with the coastal ports.

Veryan is famous for its five round houses, each surmounted by a cross; they are said to have been built this way so that the Devil could not find a corner in which to hide.

Truro lies at the head of one of the branches of the Fal estuary. It used to be an important inland port, but was unable to compete with the deep water anchorage and extensive docks of Falmouth. However, Truro's heritage is commemorated with the custom of presenting its incoming mayors with a pair of small silver oars as a representation of the city's ancient authority over the river and shipping.

The heart of Truro is Boscawen Street, laid out in its present form in the 1790s and named after the Boscawen family of Tregothnan, long-time benefactors of the town. Lemon Street in Truro gets its name from the Lemon family, who owned the land at the time of its development in the early 19th century.

VERYAN, THE ROUND HOUSES c1955 V3046

TRURO, UPPER LEMON STREET 1890 24132

When Upper Lemon Street in Truro was built in 1795 it was considered the wonder of Cornwall (see photograph 24132, above), and it is still recognised as one of the finest examples of a complete Georgian street in England. From its junction with Boscawen Street it sweeps up to the Lander Monument, which commemorates the two Truro explorer brothers, Richard and John Lander, who traced the source of the River Niger in Africa in 1827. The statue on the top is of Richard Lander, who named an island on the River Niger 'Truro'.

Cornwall was once part of the Church of England Diocese of Exeter in Devon, but in 1876 it was granted its own diocese – that of Truro. Construction of the new cathedral, the first to be built in England for 800 years, began in 1880 and continued for thirty years. City status was granted to Truro in 1877.

Falmouth's parish church of King Charles the Martyr is one of only five of that name in the country. In 1661 Charles II granted Sir Peter Killigrew the town's charter on condition that a church was built and dedicated to his father, Charles I, executed by order of Parliament in 1649. The church has an unusual rectangular tower.

Did You Know?
CORNWALL
A MISCELLANY

Falmouth sits at the entrance to the great waterway of Carrick Roads, into which the Rivers Fal, Truro and Tresillian empty their waters. No major settlement existed here before the 17th century. Although Henry VIII recognised the importance of the Carrick Roads and fortified Pendennis Point and its opposite number at St Mawes with a castle, it was not until the early 17th century that Falmouth began to grow, reputedly at the suggestion of Sir Walter Raleigh who convinced Sir John Killigrew of Arwenack House of the area's potential as a port and harbour. One of the early settlements that grew into modern Falmouth was the oddly-named Penny-come-quick. The name comes from the Cornish 'Pen-y-cuik', meaning 'the head of the creek'.

TRURO, BOSCAWEN STREET 1912 64732

In 1688 Falmouth was chosen as the base for the boats of the Post Office 'Packet' Service. As well as official mail and Royal messages, these fast brigantines carried passengers and small, expensive cargoes such as bullion, plying their rapid trade to Europe and the Americas from Falmouth. The Packets needed supplies and repairs, and their crew and passengers needed places to stay; thus two of the industries that Falmouth still relies upon – ship repairs and hotels – came into being. The Packet service came to an end in the mid 19th century, but its important place in Falmouth's history is recalled in the name of its local newspaper – 'The Falmouth Packet'.

Opposite the Post Office in Falmouth a precipitous flight of 111 stone steps scales the hill from the town's square to Vernon Place. Known as Jacob's Ladder, it was built in the 1830s by the builder and tallow-chandler Jacob Hamblen to create a direct, if somewhat exhausting, route between his shop and house.

Whilst staying at the Greenbank Hotel in Falmouth in 1907, the author Kenneth Grahame wrote the first two of a series of letters to his son that became the children's book 'The Wind in the Willows'. Reproductions of those letters are displayed in the hotel, as well as Florence Nightingale's signature in the hotel register – the pioneer of modern nursing stayed at the hotel in 1910, shortly before her death in the same year.

Penryn's prosperity in the 19th century largely derived from its granite quarries, and Waterloo Bridge, the Old Bailey and New Scotland Yard in London are all built of fine-grained Penryn granite – as is the clock tower of its Town Hall, seen in photograph 27649 (opposite). On Sundays the bell in the tower is sounded to summon worshippers, including those of Falmouth, whose Mayor and Corporation still pay £3 annually to the vicar of Penryn for the people of Falmouth to have the right to worship in their own church instead of that at Penryn.

The Lizard is the name of the peninsula of land south of Helston and the Helford River; the name is thought to derive from 'Lazar', an old word for lepers (people afflicted with leprosy), who had to live in isolated communities away from the rest of the population. The Lizard is famous for its unique serpentine rock, which assumes rich colours when it is polished and has been compared to the sinuous skin of a snake. Since the mid 19th century the serpentine stone has been turned and formed into a variety of gift objects, such as model lighthouses, and even furniture.

The Marconi Memorial on the cliff above the sea near Mullion on the Lizard commemorates the first radio signal sent across the Atlantic on 12th December 1901, when the Morse letter 'S' was transmitted from here to St John's at Newfoundland. Cornwall was also in the forefront of pioneering communication systems in the 1960s, when the GPO built a satellite station at Goonhilly on the Lizard. On 11th July 1962 the first transatlantic picture was transmitted from the main dish here via the Telstar satellite. It was followed on 13th July 1962 by the first satellite telephone message.

21

Helston was once an important Stannary town with its own coinage hall – hence the name of its Coinagehall Street. The coinage hall stood in this street until the early 1800s, and was the scene of the twice-yearly coinage sessions, when local mine-owners brought their tin into the town for assay and auction. The term 'coinage' derives from the French word 'coin', meaning corner – a piece of the ingot would be cut from the corner for assaying, when the quality of the tin would be checked.

The Loe Pool near Helston is the largest freshwater lake in Cornwall. It is separated from the sea by the great sandbank of the Loe Bar. By an ancient custom the Bar was cut to lower the water level whenever it threatened to flood Helston.

**HELSTON, COINAGEHALL STREET
1913** 65941

HELSTON, THE FURRY DANCE H69402

Hundreds of years ago a fiery dragon flew over Helston, dropping a large stone on what is now Angel Yard and frightening the population out of their wits. However, no one was hurt and the people celebrated their narrow escape by dancing in and out of each other's houses. So runs the legend of the origins of Helston's famous Furry Dance, held each May as part of the town's Flora Day celebrations to greet the arrival of summer. The name of the dance is believed to derive from the Cornish word 'feur' for a holiday, or fair. The 8am Hal-an-Tow dance involves adults and children carrying branches and singing 'Summer is come O, and Winter is a gone O'. The children's dance at 10am is a relatively new addition, first danced in 1922. The principal dance is at midday, when men dressed in top hats and tails and women in formal gowns dance in a weaving procession in and out of the town's shops, houses and gardens, accompanied by the Helston Town Band and cheered on by thousands of onlookers.

A MISCELLANY

St Michael's Mount, a tiny island offshore from Marazion near Penzance, became a place of pilgrimage after a fisherman saw a vision there of St Michael; a Benedictine priory was built on its summit in the 12th century, and Marazion grew up as a settlement catering for the pilgrims who came here. In the 17th century a fortified castle was built on the island for the St Aubyn family, who still live there.

Marazion's name is thought to derive from 'marghas byghan', Cornish words for 'little market'. In the 19th century the area had an unusual claim to fame – John Marius Wilson's 'Imperial Gazetteer of England and Wales' of 1870-72 described the land around Marazion as being 'notable for producing a superior variety of turnip'.

ST MICHAEL'S MOUNT 1928 81087

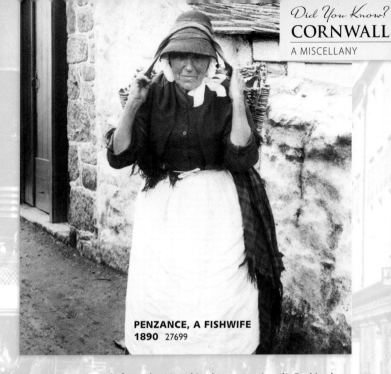

PENZANCE, A FISHWIFE
1890 27699

Mount's Bay extends from the Lizard in the east to Land's End in the west, and takes its name from St Michael's Mount. In the heyday of Cornwall's fishing industry the towns and villages around Mount's Bay had great fishing fleets. Huge pilchard shoals appeared off Land's End in July and swam along the coast to be taken in seine nets by the Mount's Bay fleets, then later in the year the boats pursued herring, followed by mackerel in the spring. The lives of whole communities revolved around catching and processing the fish – gutting, barrelling, salting and delivering. The fisher women sold their wares from 'cowels', baskets carried on their backs, which were supported by a band passed round their foreheads. They were customarily the older women, who walked for miles carrying their heavy cowels until the contents were all sold. Younger fishwives did not sell fish, but helped with the cleaning and salting of the catch.

NEWLYN, FISHERMEN 1906 56532

Mount's Bay fishermen were possessive about their fishing territory. In the infamous Newlyn Riots of 1896, 2,000 Newlyn fishermen, who never put to sea on the Sabbath Day, rioted in protest against 200 boats that had come to the area from Lowestoft and were working on Sundays. The Newlyn men barricaded the harbour, preventing the East Coast men from putting to sea, and violent fights took place between the two sides. The police could not cope, and hundreds of soldiers and a Royal Navy destroyer had to be drafted in to restore order.

In the 1880s Newlyn became famous for its artistic community, the celebrated Newlyn School of landscape painters. Its leading light was Stanhope Forbes, whose masterpiece 'Fish Sale on Newlyn Beach' can be seen in Plymouth City Art Gallery.

Life could be hard in Cornish fishing villages in the past. Failure of the fish stocks for a lengthy period could lead to problems, and it was this situation in Mousehole many years ago which gave rise to one of Cornwall's most famous traditional recipes, Stargazy Pie, in which fish are placed in a radial pattern in a pie dish with their heads resting on the rim and then covered with pastry, leaving the heads outside the pie, 'gazing at the stars'. The story goes that many years ago, during a long period of bad weather, the Mousehole fishing fleet was unable to leave the harbour, and the village was starving. One brave man, Tom Bawcock, was so concerned that he managed to put to sea and catch just enough fish to feed the village. The fish were made into a pie with their heads left on, so nothing would be wasted. Stargazy Pie is traditionally eaten in Mousehole on 23rd December, known locally as Tom Bawcock's Eve.

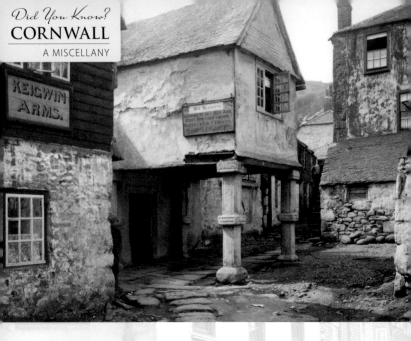

MOUSEHOLE, THE KEIGWIN ARMS 1893 31805

In July 1595 a force of Spanish soldiers landed from four galleys near Mousehole and sacked the town. The only building in Mousehole to survive the raid was the home of the local squire, Jenkyn Keigwin, who was killed defending his house. The building later became a pub, called the Keigwin Arms after its former owner, but is now a private residence that bears a plaque commemorating Squire Keigwin's fate.

The name of Penzance means 'holy headland', from the Cornish 'pen' for 'head' or 'end' and 'sans' for 'holy', which may have derived from the presence of a small chapel, dedicated to St Anthony of Padua, which used to stand on the shore near the present-day St Anthony Garden. The name of Penzance's main street, Market Jew Street, derives from the Cornish words 'Marghas Yow', meaning 'Thursday Market'.

A traditional event called 'Golowan' takes place in Penzance each year, a week-long Midsummer festival which starts on the Friday nearest to St John's Day (24th June) and culminates in Mazey Day. The festival is linked with the Feast of St John, and the name comes from the Cornish for that, 'Gol-Jowan'. It was a Midsummer celebration held all over Cornwall in the past, but was particularly popular in the Penwith area. The modern Golowan festival in Penzance is now also a major arts and culture festival, but the town is liberally decorated with greenery for the occasion, in line with the ancient tradition of Golowan.

PENZANCE, MARKET JEW STREET 1925 78635

MEN AN TOL, 1890 22986

The curious prehistoric monument known as 'Men an Tol' ('stone of the hole') stands near Madron, north of Penzance. It seems most likely that the three stones were originally part of a Neolithic long barrow (burial mound), and the holed stone was the portal through which the dead were carried. Legends and myths concerning its use abound; it is said that children were passed through the hole to cure rickets and skin diseases, and adults who were sufficiently slim could ward off fevers by crawling through the hole nine times 'widdershins' (anti-clockwise, or anti-sunwise).

The Merry Maidens stone circle near Lamorna is an early Bronze Age ceremonial site made up of nineteen granite pillars. Legend has it that the Merry Maidens are girls who were turned into stone for the sin of dancing on the Sabbath Day, as were the musicians who played for them – two standing stones north of the circle (but not visible from it) are called the Pipers, and one visible to the west (the Goon Rith standing stone) is known as the Fiddler. The circle itself is also known as the Dawn's Men, a corruption of 'Dans Maen', meaning 'stone dance'.

Photograph P273005 (below) shows the weather-beaten engine house and chimney above the old tin and copper workings of Wheal Edward at Pendeen. In the 19th century, three-quarters of the world's copper was mined in Cornwall, but then competition from mines abroad led to a slump, and few mines survived into the 20th century. The decline of the tin and copper mines led to large numbers of Cornishmen emigrating all over the world in search of mining work – they became known as 'Cousin Jacks' in their new countries, probably because they hailed each other with the greeting of 'cousin'. It used to be said that you could find a Cornishman at the bottom of any hole in the world.

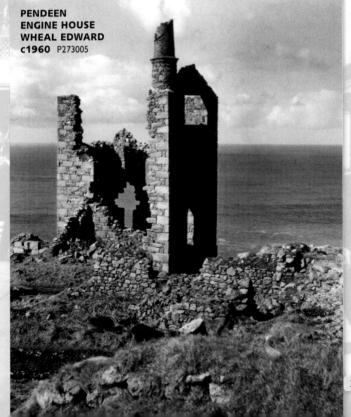

**PENDEEN
ENGINE HOUSE
WHEAL EDWARD
c1960** P273005

ZENNOR, THE MERMAID, BENCH END IN THE CHURCH Z1402

The village of Zennor is the setting for the legend of the mermaid of Zennor, who lived in nearby Pendour Cove. She was entranced by the sound of Matthew Trewella singing in the village church, and often crept ashore to listen to his lovely voice. She and Matthew fell deeply in love, but the mermaid had to return to the sea, for she could not stay long on dry land. Unable to live without her, Matthew followed the mermaid to the beach and the couple disappeared under the waves together. Matthew was never seen again, but it was said that the sound of him happily singing to his mermaid love could be heard from the cliffs above Pendour Cove. His voice would be soft and sweet if the weather was set fair, but deep and low if there was a storm brewing, and local fishermen would listen for his song before deciding whether to put to sea or stay at home for the day. There is a carving of a mermaid on one of the wooden bench ends in Zennor's church of St Senana; she holds a mirror in one hand and a comb in the other, the symbols of seduction with which these sirens of the sea were often depicted. The carving is believed to be about 500 years old, and local folklore says that it was done as a warning to other young men not to be tempted away by the charms of mermaids.

ST IVES, ON THE BEACH
1890 24178

St Ives encapsulates everything Cornish with its labyrinth of narrow, pitching streets, its broad stretches of golden sand, and its fishing fleet and harbour. St Ives fishermen favoured flat-bottomed craft that remained upright at low water in the harbour surf. Many Cornish boats had pointed sterns so that more craft could be packed like sardines into the tiny harbours west of the Lizard. The Digey area is where the town's oldest buildings survive. Here, in courtyards and open-sided cellars, was where pilchards and herrings used to be laid out or 'baulked' into piles, the layers of fish being separated by layers of salt. The combined weight forced oil out of the fish. The oil drained along channels in the stone floors and then into granite containers, and was used for numerous purposes, including lighting. Much of the fish salted in this way was packed into barrels and shipped to the Mediterranean countries, where there was a huge market for Cornish fish. St Ives was also noted in the past for its smoked herrings, or 'kippers', whose preparation in smoke houses added to the miasma of smells which scented the town. A Victorian visitor once remarked that the overpowering stench was enough to stop the town clock.

St Ives is famous now for its artistic community. Renowned artists such as Christopher Wood, Ben Nicholson, Barbara Hepworth, Peter Lanyon and Patrick Heron all lived and worked there, making use of the clear quality of the light that this area is famous for, which suits the open air style of painting. Today the St Ives Tate Gallery, a striking building above Porthmeor Beach, celebrates that artistic tradition.

On a hill overlooking St Ives is the memorial to John Knill, who left a legacy for a curious celebration to be held in his memory every five years on St James's Day (25th July). The main event is when 10 girls dressed in white, two widows, a fiddler, the parson, a customs officer and the mayor parade to the monument; the girls have to be the daughters of either fishermen, tinners or seamen, and there is great competition to be chosen. The girls dance around the monument to music played by the fiddler, then everyone sings the Hundredth Psalm before the Master of Ceremonies brings the event to an end for another five years.

The Copperhouse district of Hayle, west of St Ives, is so-named because it used to be the part of the town where there was once a copper works, later a foundry.

Gwithian Towans, the stretch of sandhills along the western side of St Ives Bay, was from 1889-1920 the home of the National Explosives works, which produced much of the cordite used in artillery shells during the First World War. It employed around 1,800 people who worked in small enclosures sunk into the dunes and isolated from each other to prevent a disastrous chain reaction in the event of an explosion or fire.

Camborne grew into the county's tin mining capital in the late 1700s, and its massive Dolcoath mine was one of the deepest mines in the world at the end of the 19th century. One of Camborne's own sons, Richard Trevithick (1771-1833), helped to create its prosperity by inventing the pump engine that drained the mines of water, enabling shafts to be sunk to deeper levels than ever before. Richard Trevithick is regarded as the father of the high pressure steam engine, and is remembered in Camborne by the annual Trevithick Day in April. He developed a steam-powered locomotive called 'the Puffing Devil' which he exhibited in 1801 by transporting a group of friends up Camborne Hill (Tehidy Road and up Fore Street), making 'the Puffing Devil' one of the world's first passenger-carrying road vehicles. The main event of the Trevithick Day celebrations is a parade of several dozen steam engines through the streets of the town as they recreate Trevithick's first steam engine journey of 1801, an event also commemorated in the Cornish folksong 'Camborne Hill'.

CAMBORNE, COMMERCIAL SQUARE 1902 49112

**REDRUTH, FORE STREET
1898** 41621

Redruth was also an important mining town in the past. South of
the town is the famous amphitheatre of Gwennap Pit, which was
fashioned from collapsed mine workings on the slopes of Carn Marth.
Ever since John Wesley preached there in the 18th century, it became
a venue for open-air religious services for the Non-conformist miners
and their families.

The hill of Carn Brea, south west of Redruth, is one of the sites for the
traditional Midsummer bonfires that are lit on high hills in several
parts of Cornwall on Midsummer Eve (or St John's Eve, 23rd June).
When the fires have burned down, young people jump across the
embers to drive away evil and bring good luck, a custom which dates
back to Celtic times, and perhaps even earlier.

The small port of Portreath was built to serve the mines at Camborne
and Redruth, and was once busy with ships bringing coal from South
Wales and returning with copper ores for the smelters of Swansea.
It was the terminus of Cornwall's first (horse-drawn) railway, which
connected it with the local mines.

Perranporth takes its name from St Piran, patron saint of Cornish miners, and was originally a mining community. Around the town many old engine houses from the tin mines are prominent features in the landscape, while Wheal Towan is what is left of an old copper mine. This is 'Poldark' country: Winston Graham was living in Perranporth when he wrote the first novel in his popular Poldark family saga. His inspiration for the name of his feisty heroine was the hamlet of Demelza near St Wenn, west of Bodmin.

Harmony Cottage in Mithian, just off the St Agnes to Perranporth Road, was the humble birthplace in 1761 of the artist John Opie, who became known as the 'Cornish Wonder'. Although the son of a carpenter, his painting skills were recognised and he was taken to London, where he became a famous portrait painter and eventually a professor at the Royal Academy. He died in 1807 and was buried in St Paul's Cathedral in London – a true Cornish rags to riches tale.

**NEWQUAY, THE HUER'S HOUSE
1907** 59333

The old village stocks at Crantock, near Newquay, are now preserved under a shelter behind the village church, but they once stood inside the church tower, where their last occupant was William Tinney, who robbed a local widow with violence in 1817. He managed to escape the stocks, and then climbed inside the tower, cut the bell rope and used it to lower himself down outside where he made his getaway and went off to sea, never to be seen again. Behind the stocks is a carved wooden panel with a depiction of William Tinney undergoing his punishment.

Until the mid 19th century Newquay was mainly a fishing village. The building shown in photograph 59333 (opposite) was where a man called the huer would be on lookout duty for the purple stain on the sea that heralded an incoming pilchard shoal. When sighted, the huer would raise the alarm by crying 'Hevva! Hevva!' ('Here they are!') through his trumpet, or loud hailer, and use signals made with two bushes or flags to direct the fishing fleet to the shoal out in the bay. The hut offered basic accommodation for the huer, who would take up his post several days before the shoals of pilchards were expected and would live here during the hours of daylight for up to four months of the year.

Newquay's old Cornish name is 'Tewynplustri', which means 'boat cove in the sandhills'. Fishermen here had to launch their gigs through the surf directly from the beach before the harbour, or 'New Quay', was built in the 15th century. In the 1840s Newquay's harbour was bought and developed by Joseph Thomas Treffry; his mining interests lay nearer to the south coast, and he was worried by shipping losses on the treacherous passage around Land's End. Copper ores from his Fowey Great Consols mine crossed the peninsula on a tramway to Newquay, where they were loaded onto ships that took them to the smelters in South Wales.

Along the coast north of Newquay are the green-capped rocks of Bedruthan Steps. These huge foreshore stacks were formed by the erosion of softer rocks around them, but Cornish folklore says they were stepping-stones used by a giant called Bedruthan.

ST COLUMB MAJOR, FORE STREET 1906 56244

In 1549 the people of Cornwall and Devon rose up in revolt in what is known as the Prayer Book Rebellion against the introduction of the Book of Common Prayer into church services, a move to bring in the new theology of the Reformation. The Duke of Somerset was sent with an army to crush the revolt, and thousands of rebels were killed. Among them was William Mayow, the Mayor of St Columb Major, who was hanged outside a tavern in his home town for taking a leading role in the uprising.

The River Camel rises north of Camelford on the edge of Bodmin Moor, and is one of Cornwall's best salmon rivers – a 34lb specimen was caught in the 1920s.

Padstow is famous for its ancient May Day 'Obby 'Oss celebrations. The 'Oss is a man dressed in a heavy costume with snapping jaws, plumed cap and hooped skirt. He prances through the town accompanied by a Teaser, singers, dancers and musicians. The 'Oss is thought to originally have been a fertility symbol and a woman 'caught' under its skirts during the celebrations is supposed to become lucky, or pregnant.

For many years Padstow was a bustling port for transatlantic passenger ships as well as a busy fishing harbour noted for its catches of sole, but the gradual silting up of the Doom Bar outside the harbour has limited the size of the ships that can berth here. According to legend, the harbour was cursed centuries ago by a mermaid who was shot with an arrow from a longbow by a Padstow man. She cast some sand into the sea and foretold – correctly – that it would block the harbour.

At Wadebridge the River Camel is so fast-flowing that there were once chapels on each bank by the ford over the river where travellers prayed for safe crossing before venturing forward. In the late 15th century the building of the graceful but solid 17-arched bridge over the river must have been welcomed. Called the 'longest and fairest' bridge in Cornwall, this historic structure has now been bypassed by a high bridge downstream, and so is safe from the depredations of modern traffic.

Inside Padstow's parish church of St Petroc are several interesting monuments to the Prideaux family. Photograph 69708 (left) shows the monument of 1627 to Sir Nicholas Prideaux who built Prideaux Place, the castellated mansion that stands above the town, depicting him in armour with his wife and four sons.

**PADSTOW
ST PETROC'S CHURCH
THE PRIDEAUX MONUMENT
1920** 69708

Fishing was Port Isaac's main means of earning a living for centuries, but, as in many Cornish villages, local people in the past were also involved in smuggling. In this they were aided by Port Isaac's narrow streets, or 'drangs', in which they could run the excise men ragged, communicating by a series of coded knocks on the walls of adjoining houses. Nowadays Port Isaac is famous as the location for the TV series 'Doc Martin', and also as the home of the singing group 'Fisherman's Friends', who perform sea shanties and other nautical songs on the quay on Friday evenings in the summer.

PORT ISAAC, THE HARBOUR 1920 69688

The ruined castle of Tintagel on the north coast is the legendary birthplace of King Arthur. It is possible that King Arthur was a real person, perhaps a British leader who opposed the Saxon invasions of the Dark Ages, and there was great excitement in the media when in 1998 a piece of rock was uncovered at Tintagel bearing a Runic inscription dating from the 500s, which includes the name 'Artognov' or 'Arthnou'; this was promptly dubbed 'the Arthur Stone', and hailed as proof of the Arthurian connection with Tintagel. However, Dr Geoffrey Wainwright, chief archaeologist with English Heritage, said: 'Despite the obvious temptation to link the Arthnou stone to either the historical or the legendary figure of Arthur, it must be stressed there is no evidence to make this connection. Nevertheless it proves for the first time that the name existed at that time and that the stone belonged to a person of status.'

Cornwall's exposed, treacherous northern coast was so dangerous for shipping in the past that an old rhyme reminds us of its constant threat:

> *'From Padstow Point to Lundy Light,*
> *Is a sailor's grave by day or night'.*

BOSCASTLE, THE VILLAGE 1906 56169

The deep inlet of Boscastle's small harbour is one of the few safe anchorages on Cornwall's northern coast. Near the harbour mouth is a blowhole, which at certain times of the tide produces an explosive booming sound that can be heard clear across the harbour. Boscastle was the subject of a BBC TV series, 'A Seaside Parish', in 2004. The rector of Boscastle is also responsible for the church at nearby St Juliot, which was restored in the 19th century to plans drawn up by the author Thomas Hardy, who trained as an architect before turning to literature. It was whilst working here on this church that Thomas Hardy met and fell in love with his first wife, Emma Gifford, the sister-in-law of its vicar.

Camelford sits at the north-west edge of Bodmin Moor on the banks of the Camel, where there was a ford to cross the river before the bridge was built. In a witty play on the town's name, a weathercock featuring a camel crowns its fine Town Hall. West of Camelford is Delabole, where the famous slate quarry is the deepest in England, and the oldest slate mine in the world still working.

Specimens of 'Little Trees', a species of deep water coral, are sometimes washed up on the beach at Crackington Haven on the north coast. Local lore says they are a good luck charm, and that having a piece in your home will prevent it burning down.

Before the railway arrived, the present-day resort of Bude was only a seaport for the 35-mile-long Bude Canal, built in 1823. It featured hydraulic inclined planes instead of locks for negotiating changes in water level, where water-powered engines drove a chain to which each boat was attached so that it could be hauled up and down. The main business of the Bude Canal was carrying lime-rich sea sand dug from the beach to improve the acid farm soils of the hinterland. The canal was closed, except for the Bude section, in the 1890s, but the sea lock was restored to working order in 2001.

North of Bude, Morwenstow's parish church of St John the Baptist has a superb Norman north arcade with richly carved capitals and arches. Reverend Robert Stephen Hawker, Morwenstow's vicar from 1834 to 1875, introduced the Harvest Festival service here. He was also a poet and songwriter, and wrote 'The Song of the Western Men' – Cornwall's national song.

BUDE 1906 56076

SPORTING CORNWALL

A popular sport in the past in Cornwall was 'Hurling the Silver Ball', in which a ball made of apple wood encased in silver was thrown (or 'hurled') between two large teams of participants playing over a huge area, either between two goals several miles apart, or to the parish boundary. Hurling used to be widespread throughout Cornwall, but now only takes place in St Ives and St Columb Major. The Hurling the Silver Ball match that takes place in St Ives in February is played by children, but a truer version of the traditional game is played at St Columb Major twice a year, on Shrove Tuesday (Pancake Day), and the Saturday of the following week. It is played by two teams, 'Town' against 'Country'. The initial stages of the game can be stopped at any time for onlookers to touch the silver ball for luck, good health or fertility, and then the serious contest begins. The 'Town' goal is the base of an old Celtic cross and the 'Country' goal is a stone trough; the goals are about two miles apart, at either end of the town. To win, the team must carry the ball to its own goal, or alternatively carry it over the parish boundary, a distance of about 3 miles. When the ball has been goaled or carried out of the parish, the game is over, and the winner is the person who achieves this. The winner has the right to keep the silver ball, but must have a new one made to replace it for the next year's match. The game is recalled in the name of The Silver Ball pub in Fair Street in St Columb Major and on the town crest, which features a hand holding a hurling ball and the motto 'Town and Country Do Your Best'.

In 1863 the boxer Bob Fitzsimmons was born in a cottage at the top of Wendron Street in Helston, now marked with a plaque. He was the first man to be World Middleweight, World Light Heavyweight and World Heavyweight Boxing Champion, and prior to Lennox Lewis in 1993 he was the last Englishman to win the World Heavyweight boxing championship, when he defeated Jim Corbett in 1897.

CORNWALL

A MISCELLANY

Gig racing is a popular water sport in both Cornwall and the Isles of Scilly. Racing gigs developed from pilot gigs, light and manoeuvrable six-oared boats used in the past to take harbour pilots out to incoming boats. For the crews of the pilot gigs, speed was of the essence to ensure their pilot was the one that got the pillage fee, so there arose a great rivalry between crews which in time led to the sport of pilot gig racing. The Cornish gig 'Newquay', built in 1812, is still used for gig racing by the Newquay Rowing Club and is believed to be the oldest traditional rowing boat in regular use.

Cornish wrestling is a unique sport that has been popular in the county for centuries. The referee in a Cornish wrestling match is called a 'stickler', which may be the origin for the use of this word to describe someone who is a 'stickler' for the rules or correct way of doing something. Cornish wrestlers wear a tough jacket, which allow each opponent to gain a better grip on the other. All holds are taken upon the other wrestler's jacket, although the flat of the hand may be used to push or deflect an opponent. Three 'sticklers' watch and control each bout, whilst recording a score of points ('pins') achieved in play, which are scored according to the different holds achieved. The object of the bout is to throw the other opponent to lie flat on his back, a throw called a 'Back' – if this is achieved, the sticklers raise their sticks and the throwing wrestler is deemed the winner. The Cornish Wrestling Association has an exhibition tent at the Royal Cornwall Show each year, and demonstrations of the sport take place in the Countryside ring during the show.

QUIZ QUESTIONS

Answers on page 52.

1. Livestock in a Cornish village is not at all uncommon, but Gweek has some rather unusual mammalian residents – what are they?

2. What is Cornish Yarg?

3. The author Virginia Woolf was a frequent visitor to Cornwall. Which structure in Cornwall inspired the title of one of her most famous books?

4. A number of places mentioned in this book are described as being 'Stannary towns' in the past – what did this mean?

5. What place in Cornish history is held by Dolly Pentreath of Paul, near Mousehole?

6. Outside the Market House in Market Jew Street in Penzance is a statue to the town's most famous son, Humphry Davy, close to the house where he was born in 1778. What is he famous for?

7. Who were Cornwall's 'bal maidens'?

8. Where in Cornwall can you follow a Camel Trail, and what is it?

9. What in Truro are known as Victoria, Edward and Alexandra?

10. The Royal Albert Bridge across the Tamar estuary at Saltash made the first direct rail link between Cornwall and the rest of England when it was opened by Prince Albert in 1859. It is the celebrated masterpiece of which famous engineer?

ST IVES, LIFEBOATMEN 1906 56543

RECIPE

FIGGY HOBBIN

Figgy Hobbin (or Figgy 'Obbin) is a traditional recipe from Cornwall. It also known as Figgy Duff. 'Figs' is the name used in Cornwall for raisins, although currants can also be used.

225g/8oz plain flour
1 teaspoonful baking powder
A pinch of salt
115g/4oz suet
75g/3oz raisins (or currants, if preferred)
Grated peel of half a lemon
Cold water to mix
A little milk for glazing

Pre-heat the oven to 180°C/350°C/Gas Mark 4.

Mix together the flour, baking powder, suet and salt, and add enough cold water to form a stiff dough. Roll out the dough on a lightly floured surface to about 1cm (half an inch) thick, and sprinkle the raisins (or currants) and lemon peel over it.

Roll up the pastry to make a cake like a Swiss roll, then pinch and seal the ends. Make a criss-cross pattern on the top with a sharp knife, and brush with milk. Bake in the pre-heated oven for about 30 minutes, and serve hot, cut into slices, with custard or cream.

LOOE, THE OLD GUILDHALL 1906 56396

RECIPE

**TRURO, THE CATHEDRAL FROM
THE SQUARE 1938** 88956

SAFFRON CAKE

Saffron is derived from the dried and powdered stigmas of the styles of the saffron crocus. It is one of the most expensive spices, as it requires many thousands of crocus flowers to make a small quantity of saffron. It has long been a popular flavouring in both Devon and Cornwall, giving cakes or loaves a golden colour and a honey-like taste. Saffron cakes or buns were once traditionally only made at Easter.

> A good pinch of saffron threads
> 450g/1 lb strong plain flour
> ½ a teaspoonful salt
> 50g/2oz lard
> 50g/2oz butter or margarine
> 2 teaspoonfuls of fast acting dried yeast
> 75g/3oz caster sugar
> 115g/4oz currants, raisins or sultanas (or a mixture, if preferred)
> 150ml/ ¼ pint milk
> 1 egg, beaten, to glaze

Cut the saffron threads into small pieces into a bowl, and add 150ml/ ¼ pint boiling water. Cover, and leave for at least 1-2 hours – or overnight if possible – for the colour and flavour to develop.

Sift the flour and salt into a mixing bowl. Cut the lard and butter or margarine into small pieces and rub them into the flour until the mixture resembles fine breadcrumbs. Add the yeast, sugar, and dried fruit and stir it so that it is all well mixed. Make a well in the centre of the mixture.

Add the milk to the saffron and water mixture, and gently warm until it is lukewarm. Pour it into the flour mixture and mix it all together. Lightly flour your hands and knead the mixture gently until it can be gathered into a ball of dough. Cover the bowl with a damp cloth or a piece of oiled cling film, or place the bowl inside an oiled polythene bag, and leave in a warm place to rise, for about one hour.

Grease a 900g/2 lb loaf tin and line it with baking paper. Turn out the dough on to a lightly floured surface and knead it gently for a short time, then place the dough in the prepared loaf tin. Cover again, and leave to rise again for a further 30 minutes.

Pre-heat the oven to 200°/400°/Gas Mark 6. Brush the top of the loaf with the beaten egg. Bake the loaf in the pre-heated oven for 40-45 minutes, until it is risen and cooked through (cover the top with foil if the surface is starting to brown too much). Leave in the tin to settle for 15 minutes before turning out on to a wire rack to cool.

Store in an airtight container and serve sliced, spread with butter. This also makes excellent toast.

QUIZ ANSWERS

1. Seals, at the National Seal Sanctuary. It is a rescue centre for sick, injured or orphaned seals, but also has resident Grey Seals, Common Seals, Fur Seals and Patagonian and California Sea Lions for visitors to see.

2. Cornish Yarg is a unique cheese made by the Lynher Dairy at Ponsanooth. The cheese is pressed and brined before being wrapped in nettle leaves and left to ripen. The (edible) nettles give the cheese a delicious flavour as it matures.

3. Godrevey Lighthouse, off Godrevey Point on Cornwall's treacherous north coast. The white tower of the lighthouse is visible from across the bay at St Ives, and inspired Virginia Woolf's novel 'To the Lighthouse' in which a small boy is intrigued by the structure and longs to visit it.

4. A Stannary town was a place that had been given the official duty of testing the quality ('assaying') and stamping locally mined tin.

5. The last natural speaker of the Cornish language is generally held to have been Dorothy 'Dolly' Pentreath of Paul, near Mousehole. She died in 1777 and is commemorated with a memorial in the churchyard in Paul.

6. Humphrey Davy was a scientist and inventor who identified nitrous oxide, or 'laughing gas', but he is most famous for inventing a miners' safety lamp, or Davy lamp, which allowed miners to work safely in the presence of flammable gases.

7. Bal maidens were the women and girls who worked at Cornwall's mines in the past ('bal' was Cornish for 'mining place'). They were employed in large numbers from the 1770s to the 1860s and then less so, but there were still bal maidens working at the mines in the 1920s. They did not work underground but on the surface, dressing ore.

8. The Camel Trail is a cycle path that follows the line of the disused railway along the Camel estuary for 6 miles from Padstow to Wadebridge, then on another 8 miles to Bodmin. It can then be followed further up to the western edge of Bodmin Moor.

9. Truro Cathedral was built between 1880 and 1909 in the Early English style. The central tower and the twin towers of the west front are known as 'Victoria, Edward and Alexandra' (see photograph 88956 on page 50). The central, tallest, spire was named Victoria in honour of the Queen, who died in the year it was commissioned. The later twin western spires were named after Queen Victoria's successor, King Edward VII, and Alexandra, his Queen; as the Prince of Wales, Edward had laid the foundation stones of the cathedral in 1880.

10. The Royal Albert Bridge at Saltash was designed by Isambard Kingdom Brunel.

SALTASH, THE ROYAL ALBERT BRIDGE 1890 22477

FRANCIS FRITH

PIONEER VICTORIAN PHOTOGRAPHER

Francis Frith, founder of the world-famous photographic archive, was a complex and multi-talented man. A devout Quaker and a highly successful Victorian businessman, he was philosophical by nature and pioneering in outlook. By 1855 he had already established a wholesale grocery business in Liverpool, and sold it for the astonishing sum of £200,000, which is the equivalent today of over £15,000,000. Now in his thirties, and captivated by the new science of photography, Frith set out on a series of pioneering journeys up the Nile and to the Near East.

INTRIGUE AND EXPLORATION

He was the first photographer to venture beyond the sixth cataract of the Nile. Africa was still the mysterious 'Dark Continent', and Stanley and Livingstone's historic meeting was a decade into the future. The conditions for picture taking confound belief. He laboured for hours in his wicker dark-room in the sweltering heat of the desert, while the volatile chemicals fizzed dangerously in their trays. Back in London he exhibited his photographs and was 'rapturously cheered' by members of the Royal Society. His reputation as a photographer was made overnight.

VENTURE OF A LIFE-TIME

By the 1870s the railways had threaded their way across the country, and Bank Holidays and half-day Saturdays had been made obligatory by Act of Parliament. All of a sudden the working man and his family were able to enjoy days out, take holidays, and see a little more of the world.

With typical business acumen, Francis Frith foresaw that these new tourists would enjoy having souvenirs to commemorate their days out. For the next thirty years he travelled the country by train and by pony and trap, producing fine photographs of seaside resorts and beauty spots that were keenly bought by millions of Victorians. These prints were painstakingly pasted into family albums and pored over during the dark nights of winter, rekindling precious memories of summer excursions. Frith's studio was soon supplying retail shops all over the country, and by 1890 F Frith & Co had become the greatest specialist photographic publishing company in the world, with over 2,000 sales outlets, and pioneered the picture postcard.

FRANCIS FRITH'S LEGACY

Francis Frith had died in 1898 at his villa in Cannes, his great project still growing. By 1970 the archive he created contained over a third of a million pictures showing 7,000 British towns and villages.

Frith's legacy to us today is of immense significance and value, for the magnificent archive of evocative photographs he created provides a unique record of change in the cities, towns and villages throughout Britain over a century and more. Frith and his fellow studio photographers revisited locations many times down the years to update their views, compiling for us an enthralling and colourful pageant of British life and character.

We are fortunate that Frith was dedicated to recording the minutiae of everyday life. For it is this sheer wealth of visual data, the painstaking chronicle of changes in dress, transport, street layouts, buildings, housing and landscape that captivates us so much today, offering us a powerful link with the past and with the lives of our ancestors.

Computers have now made it possible for Frith's many thousands of images to be accessed almost instantly. The archive offers every one of us an opportunity to examine the places where we and our families have lived and worked down the years. Its images, depicting our shared past, are now bringing pleasure and enlightenment to millions around the world a century and more after his death.

For further information visit: www.francisfrith.com

INTERIOR DECORATION

Frith's photographs can be seen framed and as giant wall murals in thousands of pubs, restaurants, hotels, banks, retail stores and other public buildings throughout Britain. These provide interesting and attractive décor, generating strong local interest and acting as a powerful reminder of gentler days in our increasingly busy and frenetic world.

FRITH PRODUCTS

All Frith photographs are available as prints and posters in a variety of different sizes and styles. In the UK we also offer a range of other gift and stationery products illustrated with Frith photographs, although many of these are not available for delivery outside the UK – see our web site for more information on the products available for delivery in your country.

THE INTERNET

Over 100,000 photographs of Britain can be viewed and purchased on the Frith web site. The web site also includes memories and reminiscences contributed by our customers, who have personal knowledge of localities and of the people and properties depicted in Frith photographs. If you wish to learn more about a specific town or village you may find these reminiscences fascinating to browse. Why not add your own comments if you think they would be of interest to others? See **www.francisfrith.com**

PLEASE HELP US BRING FRITH'S PHOTOGRAPHS TO LIFE

Our authors do their best to recount the history of the places they write about. They give insights into how particular towns and villages developed, they describe the architecture of streets and buildings, and they discuss the lives of famous people who lived there. But however knowledgeable our authors are, the story they tell is necessarily incomplete.

Frith's photographs are so much more than plain historical documents. They are living proofs of the flow of human life down the generations. They show real people at real moments in history; and each of those people is the son or daughter of someone, the brother or sister, aunt or uncle, grandfather or grandmother of someone else. All of them lived, worked and played in the streets depicted in Frith's photographs.

We would be grateful if you would give us your insights into the places shown in our photographs: the streets and buildings, the shops, businesses and industries. Post your memories of life in those streets on the Frith website: what it was like growing up there, who ran the local shop and what shopping was like years ago; if your workplace is shown tell us about your working day and what the building is used for now. Read other visitors' memories and reconnect with your shared local history and heritage. With your help more and more Frith photographs can be brought to life, and vital memories preserved for posterity, and for the benefit of historians in the future.

Wherever possible, we will try to include some of your comments in future editions of our books. Moreover, if you spot errors in dates, titles or other facts, please let us know, because our archive records are not always completely accurate—they rely on 140 years of human endeavour and hand-compiled records. You can email us using the contact form on the website.

Thank you!

For further information, trade, or author enquiries
please contact us at the address below:

The Francis Frith Collection, Oakley Business Park, Wylye Road, Dinton, Wiltshire SP3 5EU England.
Tel: +44 (0)1722 716 376 Fax: +44 (0)1722 716 881
e-mail: sales@francisfrith.co.uk **www.francisfrith.com**